D1611869

The material was previously published in the book
*The Prairie Girl's Guide to Life, how to sew a sampler
quilt & 49 other pioneer projects for the modern girl*
(ISBN 978-1-56158-986-9)

First published in this format 2013

Inspiration for hands-on living®

The Taunton Press, Inc.,
63 South Main Street,
PO Box 5506,
Newtown, CT 06470-5506
e-mail: tp@taunton.com

Jacket/Cover design: Kim Adis
Interior design and Layout: Chika Azuma

Threads® is a trademark of The Taunton Press, Inc.,
registered in the U.S. Patent and Trademark Office.

The following names/manufacturers appearing in
Prairie Girl Sewing are trademarks: DMC®, Ultrasuede®,
Pottery Barn®, Crate and Barrel®

Library of Congress Cataloging-in-Publication Data
TK

Printed in the United States of America
10 9 8 7 6 5 4 3 2 1

TABLE OF CONTENTS

THE SPIRIT OF LAURA LIVES ON

LIKE ANY GOOD FARM STOCK, I can't let my hands lie idle. But because I am a writer living in the big city, I lack the hard physical labor that would offer me a good night's sleep. My mind races when I climb under my grandmother's quilt, perhaps because I feel that I could have accomplished more that day. Perhaps my busy mind is just matching the pace of my busy hands.

It was the knitting that pulled me back, and the sewing that sealed the deal. These skills reconnected me with not only my past—reading Laura Ingalls Wilder books as a kid in farm country—but also the rich legacy of women. It's so gratifying to give a handcrafted item as a gift. The shawls that I wrap carefully with paper and sachets may become heirlooms for future generations. Also, I admit that I enjoy the compliments I receive from strangers and friends alike when I wear a hand-made garment. These days, I value a pink cabled cardigan that took me a year to knit and a quirky patterned dress more than anything else in my closet.

I never thought I'd say that.

And I never thought I'd hear it from every woman I meet these days. Gals are taking up sewing, enrolling in preserving and canning classes, checking out quilting and yarn expos, creating shrines to all things handmade. They may not realize it, but each of these women is a prairie girl.

You are a prairie girl. So get to it. After working on a meaningful prairie girl project, I guarantee you'll sleep like a baby.

HOW TO SEW A SAMPLER QUILT

〜〜〜〜〜〜〜〜〜〜〜〜〜〜〜〜〜〜〜〜〜〜〜〜〜〜

I AM A BIT OBSESSED WITH QUILTS. There, I'll admit it. As soon as I developed some taste—which was at around age 14—I spread a handmade quilt over my bed. I've never looked back. I can't afford to collect quilts but even so, I have three—two from my great-grandmother and one from my grandmother—carefully draped over a door and on the back of a chair and at the foot of my bed. They are worn in places, but they provide me with more warmth than any of my other belongings.

My good friend Susie Stevenson is my longtime craft buddy. I've followed her around to quilting expos so I could pet the amazing masterpieces on display and marvel at the many gorgeous squares of fabric. Susie was kind enough to make me a quilted pillow that now sits on the chair with my grandmother's quilt. So naturally I turned to Susie when I wanted to make something—in this case, a nine-square sampler—out of all those "fat quarters" I have accumulated.

PREPARING THE FABRIC

You are creating an heirloom, so choose cotton fabrics and thread. Polyester thread and fabrics wear differently than cotton and, after 100 years, may look oddly bright against your cotton pieces.

You are going to make a nine-square sampler. To do this, you will sew three rows of three squares together on the front of your sampler (to create a larger square) and a neutral piece of fabric to back your design (muslin is a great choice).

Keeping this in mind, select a combination of light and dark fabrics so they contrast when placed next to each other. Think of a checkerboard or a tic-tac-toe grid. For the top row, you might place dark/light/dark squares next to each other. The center row would have light/dark/light. The third and bottom row would have dark/light/dark.

Choose five squares of the same dark fabric and four squares of the same light fabric, or you could choose five different fabrics and patterns with the same color value (i.e., dark) and four different light fabrics. This works great for scraps. If you are using cut-up clothing, choose cotton fabrics and press them before using.

Once you have the fabrics for the front of your sampler, cut them into 3½-inch squares. This will give you 3-inch squares with a ¼-inch seam allowance on all sides.

For backing, cut a muslin or cotton fabric into an 11½-inch square.

PIECING THE NINE-SQUARE

On a flat surface, arrange your nine pieces how you want them to appear. Thread a needle with 2 feet of cotton sewing thread, knotting one end (or forgoing a knot altogether). With a pencil, lightly draw a line ¼ inch from each edge on the wrong side of the light squares. You are now ready to sew.

Pick up the top left and top center pieces, and sew them together using a running stitch (illustration lower right), as small and even as you can. A running stitch is super easy: Go up and down through the fabric and, in this case, accumulate several stitches on your needle before you draw the needle and thread through the cloth (it saves time).

You want to sew the pieces with a straight ¼-inch seam, so pin the pieces together if necessary. Pick up the top right piece and sew it to the center piece, on the opposite side of the top right piece (you are creating a strip three squares long). Sew the middle and bottom rows in the same fashion.

Press the seams on the back of each strip. A rule of thumb is to press toward the dark pieces so that when you sew all the strips together, the seams dovetail with each other. Using a small running stitch, sew the three rows together, again using a ¼-inch seam allowance (draw a light pencil line on the wrong side of one strip). You have now finished piecing a nine-patch quilt block by hand. Doesn't it look charming?

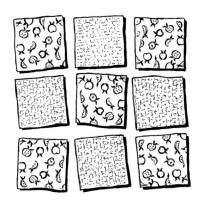

Arrange the squares

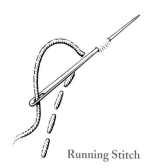

Running Stitch

TIP 👉 *If you want to hang your quilt, sew small loops of fabric onto the backing. You can run a small rod or pole through the loops and then hang it, or you can use nails or push pins on the loops to secure your work to a wall.*

ASSEMBLING YOUR SAMPLER

Now it's time for a backing. Your muslin backing should be at least 1 inch larger than the block (9½ by 9½ inches) on all sides, which in this case would make the backing 11½ by 11½ inches.

Cut out batting (you can use quilt batting or even an old blanket or piece of flannel cut to 11½ by 11½ inches). Place the backing on a flat surface, wrong side up, and tape it down so it's flat but not stretched out. Place your batting on top of this, then place your quilt block face up on top. You have created a batting sandwich of sorts. Now, using safety pins, pin through the center of each square, and through all three layers. Remove the tape.

QUILTING YOUR WORK

To turn your nine-patch block into a real quilted piece, you have to stitch through all three layers in a free-form or structured design. Switching to hand-quilting thread (which is thicker than sewing thread) and using your trusty running stitch again, follow the seams, or quilt ¼ inch in from the seams for echo squares. You can stitch Xs and Os, flowers, curvy lines, whatever you fancy. For a more structured design, trace around a template, marking your work temporarily with soap or dressmaker's chalk. The important thing is to stitch through all three layers with small stitches to create a quilted effect.

BINDING THE EDGES

To get rid of all raw edges, fold the backing—you should have an extra inch all around—over the front of your work. Tuck the raw edges under, and pin the backing down all the way around your sampler on the right side using straight pins. Pin the corners so they come to a point. To do this, sew one edge all the way to the corner. When you turn the corner to sew along the adjoining side, fold the corner over the previous sewn-down edge so it's flush and at a 90-degree angle. Examine your pinning to ensure that the edging looks even all the way around. All four sides should have the same allowance. Using a small, even stitch, sew through the nine-patch—not the batting or backing layer—to secure. You do not want these stitches to show through to the back. Continue to sew all the way around, knotting and securing your thread. That's it!

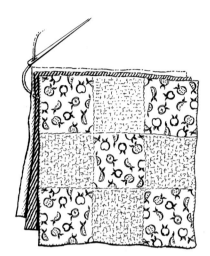

Sew through the nine-patch

TIP ☞ *Label your work. It may not seem like it now, but you are creating an heirloom. Let future generations know at whose hands this work was wrought.*

HOW TO EMBROIDER A PILLOWCASE

EVERY SELF-RESPECTING PIONEER GIRL knows she must master embroidery; after all, she has to embellish linens and lace for her hope chest. It's never too early to start planning for your future home or decorating your current homestead. Embroidery is portable and relatively easy, and it's a cheap way to decorate your linens and your clothing, with a down-home brand of chic.

Sit near a window on a quiet, sunny afternoon, bend over your embroidery hoop, and channel that frontier woman who diligently worked to make everything around her beautiful. For sweet dreams, embroider your pillowcases with of wagon wheels or sprightly green beans. (The designs and techniques here are from embroidery instructor and graphic designer Alicia Freile, who creates and embroiders her own line of handbags.)

Unless you're able to embroider free-form, you will need a pattern to follow. You can draw a rough outline of a design onto your cloth with chalk or pencil, or you can trace a pattern onto it with carbon paper, much like a seamstress would do when transferring a pattern onto fabric. You can always buy iron-on transfers, but I've supplied a couple of prairie-worthy design inspirations to try. Here's how to get a design onto fabric.

You'll need carbon paper, the kind used for patternmaking (available at craft and fabric stores). Trace the image onto the fabric by slipping the paper, face down, between the design and the back of the fabric.

Another option is to use a transfer pencil. Using the illustrations in this book as inspiration, draw a wagon wheel or string bean to create a template. Trace over your design template with the transfer pencil (note that this won't work with lettering, as the design will be reversed on the fabric when transferred). With the design face up, place the back of the fabric on top of the design on a flat surface and lightly iron. The design should be transferred onto the fabric.

Now it's time to make your fabric taut. Separate the two embroidery hoops from each other. Lay your fabric so your design is within the inner, non-adjustable hoop. Place the adjustable hoop over and around these, and press down. Make sure the top hoop is not too tight, or you may tear the fabric. Pull your fabric taut like a drum, and tighten the hoop's screw. Retighten and readjust the fabric and hoop as needed as you embroider. Whenever you put down your work for any long periods of time, loosen the screws and let your embroidery breathe.

Patience was an applied virtue on the frontier, but it is harder to achieve and maintain in these modern times. Take a breath, make a pot of tea, and begin to embroider.

Cut a piece of embroidery floss about 12 inches long (if you use a really long strand for the whole design, your floss can become tangled or simply unwieldy) and thread it through your needle. Pull a few inches through (enough so that your floss won't come off the needle while you're working), and make a knot an inch or two from the longer end.

Starting from the back of your fabric (which should feature your design tracing), bring your needle through the fabric from back to front and pull the floss through until the knot touches the fabric. Pass the needle back through the fabric, staying on the tracing. Hurray! You've just embroidered your first stitch!

It may not look like much, but your artistry will quickly be revealed as your design takes shape. There are two main stitches you need in your crafty arsenal, and you can use either to create your rolling wagon wheel or snappy green bean design.

The basic stitch is called a **backstitch** (see the illustration at left). The embroidered piece will look as if you have laid each stitch end to end. It's called a backstitch because you are embroidering backward. Let me explain.

Backstitch

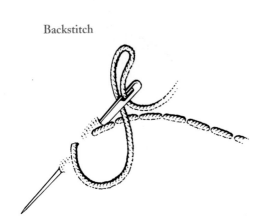

To make this tidy and speedy stitch, pick up your needle. Remember you've just made one stitch and your needle should be on the underside of your fabric. Following the tracing, poke the needle through the fabric about a ½ inch away from the first stitch and bring it up to the front of the piece. There should be a gap between your first stitch and where your needle is. You need to close the gap to create a seamless line to your design. Pass the needle down into the fabric right next to (or even into the actual hole of) your last stitch. See? You have a continuous line of embroidery floss. Continue in this manner until you reach the end of your design or you run out of floss.

A **split stitch** (see the illustration at right) works in a similar way but you take it even further. I like using split stitches because it creates more of a three-dimensional texture to the design and makes the tracing look lush and full. To create a split stitch, you will be "splitting" the floss with your needle. Your floss is made of several strands (or plies). If using a six-strand embroidery floss, you will want to pass your needle between the six plies, with three on each side.

Okay, so you've made your first stitch and your needle is on the back of your fabric. Bring the needle up through the middle of the first stitch, so the needle divides the floss in two. Now make a short stitch (use your own judgment for what constitutes "short," usually ½ inch), bringing your needle down through the fabric, making sure that you are staying

Split Stitch

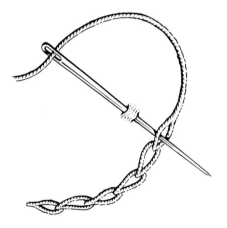

on your tracing. Continue in this fashion, splitting the previous stitch with each new one you make.

If you are about to run out of floss or reach the end of your design, leave a short tail for your first length of floss (on the back of your fabric, of course), then rethread your needle with a new piece of floss. Knot the loose strand as close to the fabric as you can. When you've completed your design, secure the stray strands: On the backside of the fabric, lay the loose strands over the line of your embroidery and whipstitch (see p. 23) around the loose embroidery floss and embroidered stitches, taking care not to pass the needle through the pillowcase fabric so it won't show on the front. When everything has been secured, weave the remaining thread back and forth through some of your stitches on the back of your fabric. Knot and trim the remaining floss.

Now that you have the tools to embellish just about anything, let's embroider some pillowcases and start filling your hope chest with lovely linens.

THE MODERN PRAIRIE GAL WAY

Any prairie lass worth her weight knew how to knit, sew, and embroider. She knitted mittens for Christmas gifts, added embroidered edging to a skirt or petticoat, and kept warm with handmade mufflers and hats. Once you've got the hang of embroidering, consider adding a trim to a skirt, or stitching a flower on your lapel, prairie chic style. There are all sorts of ways to incorporate your handicrafts into your everyday accessorizing. And let's not forget about the pleasure and thriftiness of making gifts for others. In true frontier fashion, consider making all sorts of handmade gifts throughout the year to give at holiday time.

FOR WAGON WHEELS

You can adorn your pillowcase with one or a whole string of wheels. Consider spacing them out evenly so you have an entire caravan of wagon wheels gracing your linens. And when your man tries to bring a wagon wheel coffee table into the house, you just tell him you're already full up.

If you want an extra touch of color, add some blades of green grass along the bottom of the wheel. Giddyup!

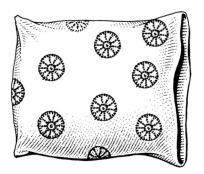

FOR GREEN BEANS

I like the idea of sprinkling various-size green beans all over pillowcases. Maybe you will dream of hunky farmers selling their wares at a county fair or outdoor market. Or just sparingly edge the pillowcase with one bean or two for an unexpected punch of color in your prairie pad.

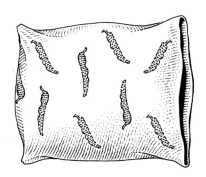

Slick: to fix or dress up.
"Belinda got slicked up for the ice cream social, hoping she'd see George."

HOW TO EMBROIDER TOWELS

THERE WERE TWO KINDS OF TOWELS IN my house: the towels we used and the towels we hung on the rack when guests came, and never the two would meet. The towels we used were usually threadbare and faded from repeated washings. But the guest towels! They were stitched with flowers, mushrooms, or holiday wreaths, all worked in metallic thread. They had fringe that looked neat and uniform, not mangy and gap-toothed. Mom sometimes got creative and folded a guest hand towel on the basin next to the dish of tiny guest soaps.

I decided to make my own adorable embroidered towels for my very own use, choosing a design that was appealing to me. You, too, can embellish your own towels, or use the delightful haystack design to spruce up curtains, handkerchiefs, clothing, or place mats.

Follow the basic instructions for embroidery on pages 9-13, or try the stitch pattern here to create a charming hand towel to put out for guests or just anytime you're feeling the need to spruce up your claim shanty.

Prewash your towel. Make sure you purchase one that has a smooth band suitable for embroidery. It's trickier to stitch evenly when the towel is plush.

Follow the directions on p. 9 to transfer the pattern onto your towel. Once the design is in place, make the towel taut by first separating the two embroidery hoops. Lay the towel so the design is within the inner, nonadjustable hoop. Place the adjustable hoop over and around these, and press down. Pull your fabric taut like a drum, and tighten the hoop's screw. Tighten and readjust the fabric and hoop as you embroider. Whenever you put down your work for any long periods of time, loosen the screws and let your embroidery breathe.

Cut a piece of floss about 12 inches long (one long strand can become tangled or unwieldy), and thread it through your needle. Pull a few inches through (enough so that your floss won't come off the needle), and make a knot an inch or two from the longer end.

Starting from the back of your fabric (which should feature your design tracing), bring your needle through the fabric from back to front and pull the floss through until the knot touches the fabric. Staying on the tracing, pass the needle back through the fabric ¼ to ⅛ of an inch away from your knot. Hurray! You've just embroidered your first stitch.

For this project, you will use a **chain stitch** (p. 16). Bring the floss to the right side (the side that you want to show) of the towel. Assuming you are holding the needle in your right

WHAT YOU WILL NEED

Size 18 to 22 embroidery needle (any size sharp needle will do, as long as you can thread embroidery floss through it and pass it through your towel)

Cotton embroidery floss

4- to 7-inch embroidery hoop

Small pair of sharp scissors

Hand towel with a smooth band (pass your needle through the fabric before beginning to make sure that the weave is not too tight)

Dressmaker's carbon paper with pencil, or transfer pencil

Seven by nine: something or someone of inferior or common quality, originating from common windowpanes of that size.
"The handwork on Lily's towel was very seven by nine, and her mother suggested she have it remade."

hand, hold the floss down with your left thumb as you stitch into the same hole you just came out of. Do not pull tightly. Instead, leave a small loop of floss on the right side of the towel. Bring the needle up through the fabric about ⅛ inch forward on your tracing, coming up through the loop. Bring the floss over the loop, and create another loop that overlaps the previous one (see the illustrations below). Continue in this manner until you finish your design. If you run out of floss, leave a tail long enough to weave through the back of your stitches when done. Change floss colors as necessary, threading the needle and knotting the floss just as you did initially.

Huckleberry above a persimmon: a cut above.
"Sam thought Minnie's pie was a huckleberry above a persimmon, but he couldn't bring himself to tell her so."

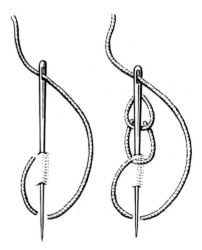

Chain Stitch

HOW TO SEW A DRAWSTRING BAG

I WAS MORE THAN SLIGHTLY OBSESSED with my mom's purse when I was growing up. It was filled with strange and wondrous things, from lipstick and cigarettes to pamphlets and pay stubs. Her wallet had cards of all sorts. I wanted a wallet badly. Somehow, those cards—all imprinted with her name—lent her an air of worth. The world knew she existed. She mattered.

Mom's purse was built for wear. To this day, she dumps all her change in the bottom of the bag, not bothering to throw it in a coin purse. When I was 10, it didn't seem a big deal to help myself to a buck or so of coins. These days, I am still fascinated with handbags, purses, clutches, shoulder bags, and the like. But they are my own and are not weighted down with coins. Like a good prairie gal, I know how valuable every penny is. To that end, here's a cute and economical way to make an adorable drawstring pouch (courtesy of my crafty chum Wendy Sloneker), perfect for gift giving, going out, or just tucking away a lip balm and spare change.

WHAT YOU WILL NEED

5½- by 14½-inch oblong piece of fabric (note that the sturdier the fabric, the sturdier the pouch)

Thread (cotton, polyester, or a cotton-poly blend)

Size 10 to 12 all-purpose sharp needle (this can depend on the type of fabric you are using)

Straight pins

2 feet ribbon or cord

Lay out the fabric

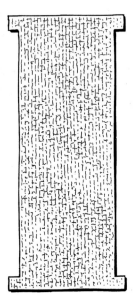

When planning your pouch, think about what you want to use it for. If you want to make a rustic bag to hold marbles or jacks, consider cutting up an old flannel shirt and pairing it with a sturdy cord. If you want a delicate pouch to use as an evening bag or a sachet, choose a dreamy organza or silk with a satin or grosgrain ribbon. Or pick a no-fray fabric, such as Ultrasuede®, fleece, or felted items, for a nice, clean project. Use hem tape in lieu of pinning.

Lay out your fabric, right side up (the side you want to show when done). Cut the fabric so that each short end is ½ inch wider than the rest of the bag as shown in the illustration at left. Fold it in half. Pin the sides in place with a few straight pins—a straight pin every inch or so.

Thread your needle with about 2 feet of thread. Pull the thread through the needle and knot both ends together.

With the fabric inside out, sew up each side, starting at the bottom fold and working your way up. A **backstitch** (p. 10) will ensure that nothing falls out of your bag. Pass your needle through the two layers of fabric. Now poke the needle through the fabric about ½ inch away from the first stitch, and bring it up to the front of the piece. There should be a gap between your first stitch and where your needle is. Close the gap for a tight seam. Pass the needle down into the fabric right next to (or even into the actual hole of) your last stitch. Continue in this manner until you reach the wider ends at the top edges.

Depending on how wide your ribbon or cord is, leave an unsewn top edge 2½ times the size of the ribbon. For instance, if your ribbon is ¼ inch wide, leave ⅝ inch of fabric at the top edge. Make sense?

Next, lay your ribbon across the unsewn top edge (see the illustration below). Fold the top flap over the ribbon and pin the edge in place. At this point, gently pull the ribbon that peeks out on either side toward the top fold of your flap. This will ensure that you don't accidentally stitch the ribbon to the bag. Now sew the flap down across the top of your pouch, leaving each end of the flap open for the ribbon to move through. Repeat this process on the other side of the pouch, sewing down the second flap of fabric and securing the ribbon inside the flap.

Lay the ribbon across the top edge

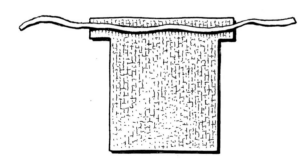

THE MODERN PRAIRIE GAL WAY

Back in the day, folks took baths once a week and it wasn't a cherished event. Pouring kettles of hot water into a metal tub in a cold kitchen isn't exactly the same experience as sinking into a bubbly bathtub in a candlelit bathroom. Sometimes they weren't able to take full baths and had to make do with cold sponge baths. These days, thank your lucky stars for the advancements in indoor plumbing and heating. Spend time luxuriating in a hot bath. Light a few votives, pour your favorite potion into the tub, and turn on some music to soothe your soul. Close your eyes and think about all the honest work you did that day. Think about your elders and how their spirit paved the way for your life. Spend some time figuring out how to downsize your life so you can fill it back up with meaningful activities. Or just lie in the tub and count your blessings, one of which is a long, hot bath.

Turn inside out. You're almost there. You can fold in the edges of the pouch where the ribbon peeks through, or permanently tuck the raw edges out of sight with a few stitches.

Knot the ends of the ribbon together. You can even string both ends through one bead and knot the two ends together. This way, you can slide the bead up to secure the closure (see the illustration to the left).

**All creation,
all nature, all wrath:**
everything or everybody.
"Covered with bruises and grass stains, Jenny's mother said the horse pulled like all creation, as it dragged her across the field."

TIP 👉 *Using thread in a contrasting color, use a blanket or whipstitch to embellish the edges of the bag.*

❋ *Use different-colored strips for your flap to create a two-tone bag.*

❋ *Sew buttons onto your pouch in a random or pinwheel design.*

❋ *Embroider metallic thread through an organza pouch or embroidery floss through a thicker fabric.*

❋ *For a kid's bag, use cork or potatoes to create a stamp and decorate the bag with fabric paints.*

❋ *Cut up an old shirt strategically, so you end up having a pocket showing on the outside of your bag.*

❋ *Make a bag on a bigger scale and use it for a laundry bag or toy sack.*

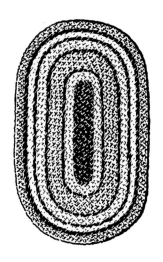

HOW TO BRAID A RAG RUG

~~~~~~~~~~~~~~~~~~~~~~~

IN A WORLD OF POTTERY BARNS® AND CRATE and Barrels®, I'm constantly upgrading my home with new bits of furniture, shelving, and crockery. But I have no desire to swap out my rugs for sisal, tufted wool, or any sort of fancy floor coverings. I'm content to putter around my home, my feet warmed by the cheery oval rag rug my grandmother made so many years ago.

Grandma's bedroom closet was filled with hat boxes, which were often stuffed with treasures other than hats. One drawer contained old greeting cards, an-other jewelry. Plastic beaded necklaces were thrown in a drawer together, creating a colorful jumble. Delicate earrings and a stylish pony pin, both crafted from Mexican silver, were hidden away in boxes, and large flower pins dotted her dressing table. Stuffed in a large plastic bag next to Grandma's bed were rags, strips of fabric she used for quilts and rugs. She used anything—worn-out work shirts, bedsheets, fabric she picked up at a rummage sale. She was always industrious. Back when my family raised chickens and other

WHAT YOU WILL NEED

Old, clean garments and fabrics

Scissors

Straight pins

Quilting thread
(available in fabric and
craft stores)

Heavy-duty needle
(a semicircular needle is helpful
but not necessary)

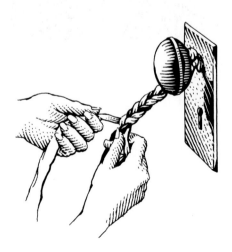

livestock, she'd go to the feed store to pick out feed bags made out of a printed cloth and make dresses out of them, throwing any remnants into the scrap bag. Like my grandmother, I hate throwing things away, especially clothes that seemed like a good idea at the time, so here's how to recycle that pink neon camp shirt from 1987 and turn it into your very own rag rug.

Gather worn clothes and fabric. Most anything will do, except for heavy fabrics like denim and thick wool. Make sure all fabric is clean. Cut off fastenings, such as buttons and zippers, and trim off pockets and the like. Cut out seams and hems; the goal is to end up with large, flat pieces of fabric.

Next, cut your cloth into 3-inch-wide strips, the longer the better. With a needle and thread, sew the short ends of the fabrics together to create long strips. Mix and match colors and patterns for a rustic rug.

The long (lengthwise) edges of your strips will be frayed. You don't want that to peek out of your braided rug, so fold the edges under about ¼ of an inch. Then fold the strip in half lengthwise, pinning in place every so often to keep the strips folded, with edges tucked inside out of sight. (If you have nimble fingers, you can also try to just tuck the edges in with your thumbs as you braid.)

Once you have three long, sewn-together, folded and pinned strips, it's time to braid. Knot the ends of the three strips together and loop them over a doorknob. (You'll trim the knotted end later.) Keep the strips taut and start braiding, just as you would hair. Make sure you remove the straight pins as you go.

When you come to the end of a strip, sew on a new length and continue to braid. When you have a good length of braid, you can start coiling your rug on a table or flat surface. For an oval rug, lay 12 inches of braid on a table and then coil the rest of the braid around it, pinning the braids to each other loosely with straight pins. For a round rug, just start coiling and pinning the braid around itself so that it spirals into an ever-expanding circle.

Using doubled quilting thread threaded through a sturdy needle, sew the braids to each other with the trusty whipstitch. To whipstitch, pull the thread through the inside braid from top to bottom, leaving about a 6- to 10-inch tail (that will be woven in later), then pull it up from the bottom to the top of the braid that butts up against it. Continue in this manner, looping or "whipping" your thread down through one braid loop and then up through the other. As you do this, work to keep the rug flat. When stitching together a sharp turn on an oval rug, the stitches on the inner braid should be closer together than the stitches on the outer braid in order to make the turn smoothly.

When the rug reaches your desired size, cut the last strips so they are narrower and braid them so the braid gradually comes to a point that will be easy to sew down and hide. Trim the ends, as well as any ends from the center that may be lurking about, such as the excess you used to hang your braid from the doorknob.

Place your rug in a place where family and friends can fully appreciate it.

Hornswoggle, honey-fuggled: to cheat; to pull the wool over one's eyes.
"Minnie was nearly hornswoggled by a merchant when she tried to buy muslin in town."

Whipstitch the braids together

Look for these other *Threads* Selects booklets at www.taunton.com and wherever crafts are sold.

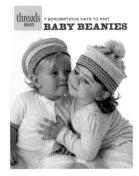

Baby Beanies
Debby Ware
EAN: 9781621137634
8 ½ x 10 ⅞, 32 pages
Product# 078001
$9.95 U.S., $11.95 Can.

Fair Isle Flower Garden
Kathleen Taylor
EAN: 9781621137702
8 ½ x 10 ⅞, 32 pages
Product# 078008
$9.95 U.S., $11.95 Can.

Fair Isle Hats, Scarves, Mittens & Gloves
Kathleen Taylor
EAN: 9781621137719
8 ½ x 10 ⅞, 32 pages
Product# 078009
$9.95 U.S., $11.95 Can.

Lace Socks
Kathleen Taylor
EAN: 9781621137894
8 ½ x 10 ⅞, 32 pages
Product# 078012
$9.95 U.S., $11.95 Can.

Colorwork Socks
Kathleen Taylor
EAN: 9781621137740
8 ½ x 10 ⅞, 32 pages
Product# 078011
$9.95 U.S., $11.95 Can.

DIY Bride Cakes & Sweets
Khris Cochran
EAN: 9781621137665
8 ½ x 10 ⅞, 32 pages
Product# 078004
$9.95 U.S., $11.95 Can.

DIY Bride Beautiful Bouquets
Khris Cochran
EAN: 9781621137672
8 ½ x 10 ⅞, 32 pages
Product# 078005
$9.95 U.S., $11.95 Can.

Bead Necklaces
Susan Beal
EAN: 9781621137641
8 ½ x 10 ⅞, 32 pages
Product# 078002
$9.95 U.S., $11.95 Can.

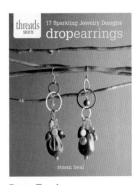

Drop Earrings
Susan Beal
EAN: 9781621137658
8 ½ x 10 ⅞, 32 pages
Product# 078003
$9.95 U.S., $11.95 Can.

Crocheted Prayer Shawls
Janet Severi Bristow & Victoria A. Cole-Galo
EAN: 9781621137689
8 ½ x 10 ⅞, 32 pages
Product# 078006
$9.95 U.S., $11.95 Can.

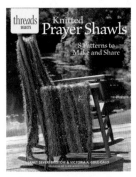

Knitted Prayer Shawls
Janet Severi Bristow & Victoria A. Cole-Galo
EAN: 9781621137696
8 ½ x 10 ⅞, 32 pages
Product# 078007
$9.95 U.S., $11.95 Can.

Shawlettes
Jean Moss
EAN: 9781621137726
8 ½ x 10 ⅞, 32 pages
Product# 078010
$9.95 U.S., $11.95 Can.